Celebrate Creation
(Kindergarten)

Written by Edith Cutting

Illustrated by Vanessa Schwab

Cover Illustrated by Kathryn Marlin

All rights reserved—Printed in the U.S.A.
Copyright © 2000 Shining Star Publications
A Division of Frank Schaffer Publications, Inc.
23740 Hawthorne Blvd., Torrance, CA 90505

Unless otherwise indicated, the New International Version of the Bible was used in preparing the activities in this book. Scripture taken from the HOLY BIBLE, NEW INTERNATIONAL VERSION. Copyright © 1973, 1978, 1984 International Bible Society. Used by permission of Zondervan Bible Publishers.

Table of Contents

To Parents and Teachers

What a fun way for children to learn all about creation! *Celebrate Creation* is filled with a wonderful variety of activities the children can do to learn about the many gifts God created for us. Children will sing songs, play games, perform finger plays, make crafts, do experiments, and draw pictures, among many other things.

The children will learn what God created on each day of creation as they complete the activities and practice such valuable skills as following directions, critical thinking, visual discrimination, coloring, sequencing, and many more. Some pages are addressed to the teacher and require adult supervision and preparation. Others can be completed by the children with your guidance.

Regardless of the kind of activity the children are working on, be sure to discuss any Bible verses presented and any aspects of the Creation story with the children. Help them come to understand that everything God created, He created out of love for all of us!

We Celebrate Creation

Read the story below and on page 5 as a whole or in parts to the children. Discuss it with them. Help them understand the great gifts God has given us.

The very, very first day that ever, ever was, was made by the Word of God. He alone made the day and the night. Always before, there had been only darkness. Darkness was over the endless deeps; darkness was all through the air. There was darkness, darkness everywhere.

Then God said, "Let there be light!" And that was the very, very first light that ever, ever was! God called the light "day," and He called the darkness "night." And that was the evening and the morning of the very, very first day that ever, ever was.

On the second day, God made the sky. He made a big, big space all around and above the water. Then He took some of the water and put it high in that space to be clouds. The rest of the water, He left down below. So there was water and sky, and dark and light. And that's all there was at the end of the second day, just water and sky, and dark and light.

Then came the third day. On that morning, God made some dry ground and separated it from the water. He called the dry ground "land," and He called the water "seas."

On that third day, God also made plants and trees to grow on the land. These were the very, very first plants and trees that had ever, ever been made. God made each one to have special seeds—different seeds, beautiful seeds—so that they would be able to grow and make more trees and plants. At the end of that third day, God looked around, and He saw that what He was making was good!

We Celebrate Creation

On the fourth day, God made special lights to shine on the day and the night. He made them different, but He made them so that there would always be some light. He made the bright, bright sun to shine all day, whether there were clouds in front of it or not. He made the paler moon to shine at night. Then He made stars and stars and stars, and He scattered them all over the sky. God gave each light a time and a place, so that it would light the day and the night, and summer and winter—year after year after year. Then God rejoiced because what He was creating was so good!

On the fifth day, God decided that living creatures should enjoy this wonderful, wonderful world that He was creating. So He made fish and other sea creatures to live in the water, and He made birds to fly up in the sky. And God saw that all He had created was good.

Then came the morning of the sixth day. What a wonderful day that was! God made animals to live on the land. He made tame animals, and He made animals to creep along the ground. He also made all the wild animals to live on the land and among the trees that He had made. Then God decided to make a man and a woman to be like Him and to manage all of the things that He had created. So He made the man and the woman, and He told them to rule over the fish of the sea and the birds of the air and the animals on the land. And He gave them all the plants and all the trees that grew on the earth. So on the evening and the morning of the sixth day, God finished making the heavens and the earth and all that is in them. And He saw that all He had made was very, very good!

At last came the seventh day. On that day, God rested from all His days of creating. Then He blessed the seventh day and made it holy.

So we celebrate God's creation: the very, very first heavens and the very, very first earth, and the very, very first plants and fish and birds and animals and people that ever, ever were.

Be Creative!

Create in me a pure heart, O God, and renew a steadfast spirit within me. (Psalm 51:10)

Explain to the children that *create* means *to make something.* Tell the children that if they paint a picture, it is their creation. If they make up a story, it is their creation. Even though God made much, much bigger and more beautiful things than we can, we can still make many wonderful things.

Teach the children the song below about creating.

If You Like to Create New Things
(Tune: "If You're Happy and You Know It")

If you like to paint a picture, clap your hands.

If you like to make a song, clap your hands.

If you like to model clay,

    Make a new thing every day,

If you like to create new things, clap your hands.

If you like to make some cookies, stomp your feet.

If you like to say a poem, stomp your feet.

If you like to build a box

    Or a tower with your blocks,

If you like to create new things, stomp your feet.

A Celebration of Creation

How lovely is your dwelling place, O Lord Almighty! (Psalm 84:1)

Below is a song that you can teach the children in parts as they learn about creation.

(Tune: "The Bear Went Over the Mountain")

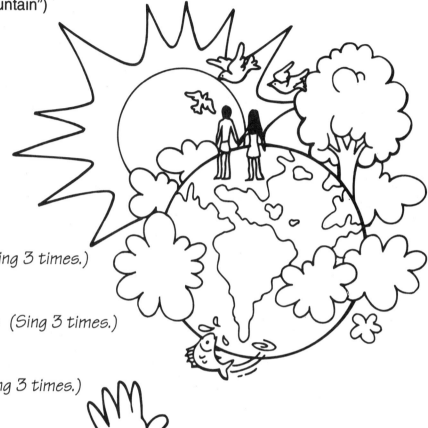

We celebrate creation.
We celebrate creation.
We celebrate creation
When God first made the light.

We celebrate creation.
We celebrate creation.
We celebrate creation
When God made day and night.

We celebrate the land and sea *(Sing 3 times.)*
God spread 'round you and me.

We celebrate the plants and trees *(Sing 3 times.)*
On land beside the seas.

We celebrate the sun and sky *(Sing 3 times.)*
And moon and stars so high.

We celebrate the fish and birds *(Sing 3 times.)*
That live in the sea and sky.

We celebrate the animals *(Sing 3 times.)*
That live upon the land.

We celebrate the people *(Sing 3 times.)*
Made just as God had planned.

We celebrate the seventh day *(Sing 3 times.)*
When we can rest and pray.

We celebrate creation *(Sing 3 times.)*
And all God made each day.

SS48835

Little Lights

Based on Genesis 1:1–5

I will lie down and sleep in peace, for you alone, O Lord, make me dwell in safety. (Psalm 4:8)

People have learned to make smaller lights since God first made all light. Circle the pictures of things people have made that give us light.

Say this prayer to thank God for making light:

Dear God, we thank You for the light,

And for the darkness, too.

We like the light

That shines so bright,

As we sleep in dark the whole night through.

Thank You!

SS48835

A Super Sky

Based on Genesis 1:6–8

From the rising of the sun to the place where it sets, the name of the Lord is to be praised. (Psalm 113:3)

Read Genesis 1:6–8 to the children. Remind them that on the second day, God made the sky. Ask what they see when they look out into God's sky. Then let them make their own skies.

Materials Needed:

sheets of light blue construction paper

cotton balls

paste

Directions:

Help each child arrange puffy clouds of cotton in his or her blue sky. Display them on windows or a bulletin board. After the children have made their skies, let them try the action rhyme below.

Blue and White Action Rhyme

What do I see

Up in the sky?

(Circle a hand around each eye as if looking through binoculars.)

White, white clouds

In a blue, blue sky!

(Circle arms as if shaping a big cloud, then spread them wide to indicate sky.)

Out in Space

This activity helps children understand what is in God's sky.

Materials Needed:

large pictures of men on the moon

pictures of earth as seen from space

Directions:

Discuss with the children people who go out in space. Tell them people do this to try to understand more of what God has made. Be sure they understand that there were no people created when God first made space. Even the moon wasn't there yet. Remind them of the big "expanse" God made.

Super Sky and Super Sea

Based on Genesis 1:6–10

Mightier than the thunder of the great waters, mightier than the breakers of the sea—the Lord on high is mighty. (Psalm 93:4)

Sky High Action Rhyme

Read Genesis 1:6–10 to the children. Talk about how God made the sky and the sea. See if the children can tell you things they see in the sky or know about the sky. Then see if they can tell you what lives in the seas.

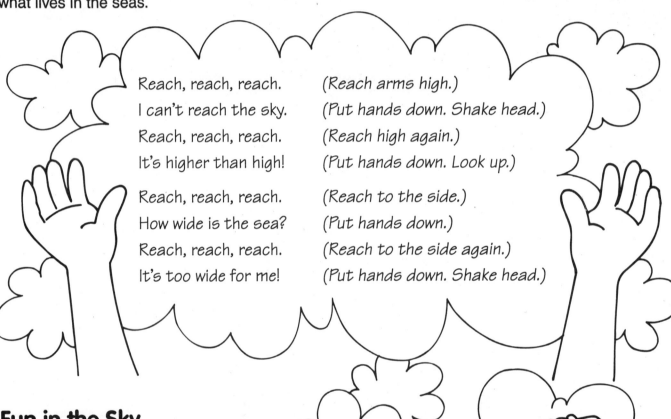

Reach, reach, reach. (Reach arms high.)
I can't reach the sky. (Put hands down. Shake head.)
Reach, reach, reach. (Reach high again.)
It's higher than high! (Put hands down. Look up.)

Reach, reach, reach. (Reach to the side.)
How wide is the sea? (Put hands down.)
Reach, reach, reach. (Reach to the side again.)
It's too wide for me! (Put hands down. Shake head.)

Fun in the Sky

Children love to look at clouds. Take them outside. Give each child a sheet of paper and a crayon or pencil. Let them sketch clouds they see. Discuss what shapes the clouds in the sky look like.

"Sea" What I "Sea"

Give each child a sheet of light blue paper. Then provide sponges cut in shapes of sea creatures (fish, sharks, whales, octopi, etc.). Children can dip the sponges in shallow tins of paint to create underwater scenes.

An Awesome World

Based on Genesis 1:9–10

He set the earth on its foundations; it can never be moved. (Psalm 104:5)

Making Land

Read Genesis 1:9–10 to the children. Talk about land with them. Discuss the different types of land there are.

Materials Needed:

a large tub or basin filled one-fourth of the way with sand, gravel, and perhaps even a few small stones

water to make the basin half full

a large empty tub or basin

Directions:

Have children scoop out the sand, gravel, and stones using their hands and put this "land" in the second basin, leaving the "seas" in the original basin. Discuss with the children how hard it is to get everything separated, what a big job it would be to separate whole seas, times they have been to the beach and played in the sand, times they have seen waves coming in on the beach, etc.

Around the World

Show the children a globe. Explain to the children that the globe represents the whole earth, and that all areas colored blue are seas. Let the children turn the globe and examine the areas. Point out the place where they are located. Show them places where they have relatives living or places that they have heard their parents speak of. Show them how small the land area is compared to all the seas. Show them how huge the world God made is, compared to the one little place where they live.

Growing Seeds

Based on Genesis 1:11–13

The desert and the parched land will be glad; the wilderness will rejoice and blossom . . . (Isaiah 35:1)

Read Genesis 1:11–13 to the children. Then try the experiment below with them to help them better understand how plants grow from seeds.

Materials Needed (per child):

small baby food jar or jelly jar
beans or other large seeds
paper towels
sand
water

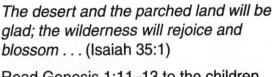

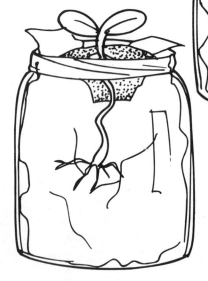

Directions:

1. Have each child line his or her jar with a piece of paper towel.

2. Help each child fill the jar with sand and then with water.

3. Place the seeds between the paper towel and the glass. This gives the seeds access to water and enables the children to see them sprout and grow.

4. Have the children water and watch the seeds frequently.

For More Fun:

Give each child a seed, a large sheet of construction paper, glue, and crayons and markers. Have them glue their seed to their paper. Then have them draw and color a picture of what they think their seed will grow into.

Fascinating Seeds
Based on Genesis 1:11–13

Sing to the Lord, for he has done glorious things; let this be known to all the world. (Isaiah 12:5)

Read Genesis 1:11–13 to the children. Then let them have fun exploring some of the plants God created and their seeds by doing the activities below.

Hidden Seeds

Materials Needed:
a variety of fruits and vegetables cut so that the seeds are exposed, spoons (optional)

Directions:

1. Tell the children that they are going to use spoons (or their fingers) to dig out seeds God made.

2. Give the children the cut-up fruits and vegetables.

3. Have them use spoons or their fingers to dig out the seeds.

4. Tell the children to put each type of seed in its own pile.

5. Have them talk about the different sizes, shapes, and colors of the seeds.

Let's Compare Seeds

Materials Needed:
bowl of large, dry, mixed seeds
  (Be sure to mark which seeds
  came from each packet.)
posterboard
packets from the seeds

Directions:

1. Have the children sort out the dry seeds that are alike.

2. Help them paste the seed packets onto the posterboard, showing pictures of the fruits or vegetables. Then they can glue the actual seeds they have sorted out next to each packet.

3. Have the children talk about the different sizes, shapes, and colors of the seeds.

Sensational Seeds

Based on Genesis 1:11–13

Give thanks to the Lord, for he is good; his love endures forever. (Psalm 118:1)

The children will have a lot of fun exploring and using seeds in the activities below.

Tasty Seeds

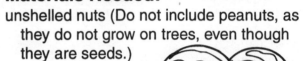

Materials Needed:

unshelled nuts (Do not include peanuts, as they do not grow on trees, even though they are seeds.)

nutcrackers

Directions:

Talk with the children about tree seeds, often called nuts. Show them samples and let the children feel them. Talk about their sizes, shapes, and colors. Shell the nuts and let the children eat a few as a snack.

Seed Designs

Materials Needed:

paper plates

glue

a variety of fairly large seeds, such as corn or sunflower seeds

Directions:

Tell the children that they are going to decorate plates with seeds. Tell them they can make any design they like (a circle around the edge like the sun or the moon, a tree, waves of the sea, etc.). Help the children understand that we can do many things with these seeds that God made so pretty and so different.

Very Good Vegetables
Based on Genesis 1:11–13

Better a meal of vegetables where there is love than a fattened calf with hatred. (Proverbs 15:17)

Read Genesis 1:11–13 to the children. Then let them try the activities below to learn about some very good vegetables God has given us. Encourage the children to try the different vegetables.

A Variety of Veggies

Materials Needed:

a variety of cut-up vegetables: carrot sticks, broccoli flowerets, radish roses, etc; a bowl of dip; a plate

Directions:

1. Let the children arrange the vegetables on the plate.

2. Talk about the vegetables with the children: where they grow, ways to eat them, which they like best, why different ones are good for them, etc. Point out the different ways these vegetables produce seeds, their colors, shapes, textures, etc.

3. Invite the children to eat the vegetables and dip for a snack.

For more vegetable fun, the children can cut out and glue pictures of all kinds of vegetables on construction paper. Or, have each child bring in a cooked vegetable. You can combine the vegetables in a pot with other ingredients to make vegetable soup.

Vegetable Prints

These works of art give vegetables a whole new purpose!

Materials Needed:

a variety of vegetables, cut up shallow tins of paint construction paper

Directions:

Give each child a sheet of construction paper. Let the children dip the cut-up vegetables in the paint to create some beautiful works of art.

Trees of All Shapes

Based on Genesis 1:11–13

Then the trees of the forest will sing, they will sing for joy before the Lord . . . (1 Chronicles 16:33)

Read Genesis 1:11–13 to the children. Then let them have fun creating all kinds of trees following the directions below.

Pipe Cleaner Trees

Materials Needed:

pipe cleaners, tape, long strip of paper (optional)

Directions:

Tell the children that God made trees in many different shapes. Ask them to use their hands to show what a tree that they remember looks like. Then have them use pipe cleaners to make a lot of different trees, talking about their shapes, sizes, etc., as they work. When the children have bent the cleaners into trees, make a forest or a double lane of trees by taping each child's tree(s) to a window or to a long strip of paper taped to the wall.

Paper Trees

Materials Needed:

green paper, scissors

Directions:

Give each child a 2" x 11" piece of green paper. Show the children how to pleat it so that there are five or six folded sections. Have each child draw a pointed or rounded treetop and a trunk on the top section, being sure to draw all the way to the folds and leaving a connected section on each fold. Have each child cut through all of the folded sections at once (leaving a connecting point on each outside folded edge). Then they can spread out their series of trees.

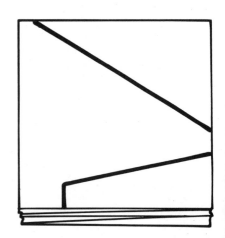

Terrific Trees

Materials Needed:

leaves collected from a nature walk, construction paper, glue, crayons

Directions:

Give each child a sheet of construction paper. Show the children how to color trunks on their papers. Then have them glue leaves they collected on a nature walk on the tops of their trees. Display them on a bulletin board.

How Trees Begin

Based on Genesis 1:11–13

He is like a tree planted by streams of water, which yields its fruit in season and whose leaf does not wither. Whatever he does prospers. (Psalm 1:3)

God made different seeds for every kind of tree. Find the ones that are alike and color them the same color. Don't color the one that is different.

17

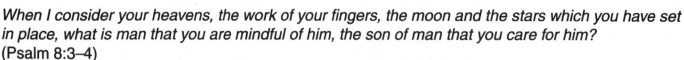

Night and Day Lights

Based on Genesis 1:14–19

When I consider your heavens, the work of your fingers, the moon and the stars which you have set in place, what is man that you are mindful of him, the son of man that you care for him?
(Psalm 8:3–4)

Read Genesis 1:14–19 to the children. Then let them enjoy making beautiful pictures representing the lights.

Materials Needed:

black construction paper
white chalk
white or pastel sheets of construction paper
crayons

Directions:

Explain to the children that after God had made the land and all the trees to grow on it, He thought again about the light He had made. He decided that there should be more than one light.

Give each child a sheet of black paper and a piece of chalk. Then ask the children to draw the lights that God made to shine at night. When they are done, have them lay those aside. Give each child a white or pastel sheet of construction paper and a variety of crayons. Ask them to draw the daytime light (sun) and what they might see during the day because it is so much brighter outside. Display the children's pictures or let the children take them home.

Shining Stars

Make copies of the star below. Every time a child does something special, give him or her one of the stars to color. Punch a hole in the top, put a piece of string through it, and give it to the child to wear.

I am one of God's special stars!

Sunshine Action Rhymes

Based on Genesis 1:14–19

Your word is a lamp to my feet and a light for my path. (Psalm 119:105)

Read Genesis 1:14–19 to the children. Then teach them the fun action rhymes below about the sun.

A Shiny Sun

The sun shines bright all day.	(Make hands frame smiling face.)
It never makes a fuss.	(Put hands down. Shake head.)
Even if we can't see the sun,	(Cover face with hands.)
The sun makes light for us.	(Smile big and spread arms.)

Our Daily Sun

The sun comes up every morning,	(Make hands frame smiling face.)
But sometimes the clouds hide its face.	(Cover face with hands.)
Whether its hidden or shining bright,	(Put hands down. Smile big.)
The sun shows how wide is God's grace.	(Stretch out arms.)

O Powerful Sun!

Never look right at the sun	(Shake head.)
For it will hurt your eyes.	(Cover eyes with hands.)
God made it the most powerful	(Raise arms with fists clenched.)
Of all the lights in the skies.	(Spread out arms.)

Merry Moon Action Rhymes

Based on Genesis 1:14–19

The heavens declare the glory of God; the skies proclaim the work of his hands. (Psalm 19:1)

Read Genesis 1:14–19 to the children. Then enjoy watching them do these simple action rhymes about the moon.

Moon Shapes

Sometimes the moon is big and round.   *(Make big circle with arms.)*

Sometimes it's just a slice.   *(With one arm still curved, fit the other arm into the curve.)*

God made it different every night,   *(Drop arms.)*

But either way, it's nice!   *(Nod and smile.)*

Our Balloon Moon

God made lots of stars.   *(Hold up one hand and point as if counting.)*

But He only made one moon.   *(Hold up only one finger.)*

It soars up in the sky   *(Move one arm in a big arc over head.)*

Like a big balloon.   *(Have both hands make a circle.)*

Big, Free Moon

Oh, what a beautiful, beautiful moon,   *(Hold up arms and have hands make a circle.)*

Floating away like a yellow balloon.   *(Keep circle while moving arms sideways.)*

If I had a string, I would pull you to me,   *(Make hand-over-hand, rope-pulling motions.)*

But God set you there so you could sail free.   *(Shake head and stretch out open hands.)*

Star Art
Based on Genesis 1:14–19

Lift your eyes and look to the heavens: Who created all these? He who brings out the starry host one by one, and calls them each by name . . . (Isaiah 40:26)

God gave us beautiful stars to light up the night sky. The children can create their own star pictures following the directions below.

Materials Needed:
black construction paper, gummed stars, pictures of constellations

Directions:
Give each child a sheet of black construction paper and a lot of gummed stars. Show the children pictures of constellations that appear in the sky. Tell them that each constellation has its own story. Let the children try to recreate a constellation that you give them, or they can make an original one about a story they have read.

Big and Little Dipper

Bright Lights Bookmarks

Based on Genesis 1:14–19

Those who are wise will shine like the brightness of the heavens, and those who lead many to righteousness, like the stars for ever and ever. (Daniel 12:3)

Read Genesis 1:14–19 to the children. Then help them create their own bookmarks.

Materials Needed:

dark felt or construction paper
gold or silver gummed stars or stickers
a sample bookmark
scissors

Directions:

Explain what bookmarks are to the children and show them some samples. Make copies of the bookmark patterns below on tagboard so the children can trace around them on the felt or construction paper. Then they can cut out their bookmarks and stick stars on them. Laminate the bookmarks if you can. Help the children find the Bible verse above and place their bookmarks there.

Star Light, Star Bright

Based on Genesis 1:14–19

. . . O morning star, son of the dawn! (Isaiah 14:12)

God gave us stars to light up the night sky. Connect the dots to create some pretty night lights. Color the picture.

Fish Fun

Based on Genesis 1:20–23

Let the sea resound, and all that is in it; let the fields be jubilant, and everything in them! (1 Chronicles 16:32)

Read Genesis 1:20–23 to the children and ask them to tell about going fishing with someone in the family. Encourage them to describe fish they have seen or caught. Help them talk about different places fish live, such as in oceans or in little brooks. Then let them try the fish activities below.

Fishbowl

Bring a fishbowl with fish in it for the children to watch. Or, take them to the home of someone who has an aquarium.

Fish Game

Tell the children that they are all going to pretend to be fish. Show them how to hold their hands with their palms together to be like a fish, and move them right and left, up and down, like a fish swimming. Tell the children to "swim" after you as you "swim" around the room, always with hands together. Explain that when you tag someone towards the end of the line, that person will become the fish leader until he or she can tag someone else.

Fish Motion Play

God made fish	(Hold hands with palms together.)
Go swish, swish, swish.	(Move hands sideways like a fish's tail.)
Big fish, little fish,	(Separate palms and stretch out arms to measure big. Then move them closer for little fish.)
Fish, fish, fish.	(Measure different sizes with hands.)

Sea Creatures
Based on Genesis 1:20–23

There is the sea, vast and spacious, teeming with creatures beyond number—living things both large and small. (Psalm 104:25)

Read Genesis 1:20–23 to the children. Tell them that they are going to pretend to be all kinds of sea creatures. Show them pictures of sea creatures other than fish. Help them to be excited and have fun so that they are not scared by the strange creatures.

Teach the children the rhyme below they can perform to learn all about God's sea creatures.

Big and Little

God made the octopus to swim	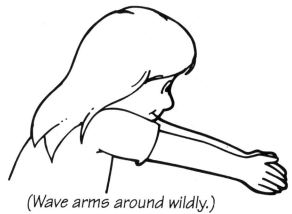
Down in the mighty ocean.	(Wave arms around wildly.)
He made the great big whale to dive	(Pretend to dive.)
And make a great commotion!	
God made the little, tiny shrimp	(Measure with thumb and finger.)
With pretty shells to hide 'em,	(Hug self.)
And then He made those hard-shelled clams	(Hold thumbs tight against fingers.)
To live down there beside 'em!	(Point down.)

All About Sea Creatures

Based on Genesis 1:20–23

Praise the Lord from the earth, you great sea creatures and all ocean depths. (Psalm 148:7)

Read Genesis 1:20–23 to the children. Explain that there are many living things besides fish in the sea. Then let them try the activities below to learn more about them.

Creature Feature

Materials Needed:

bathtub toys, such as octopi, turtles, sea horses, etc; a large pan of water

Directions:

Let the children play freely with the toys in the water. Talk about each animal's name, size, color, etc. Discuss with the children why God gave us so many beautiful sea creatures.

Seashell Fun

Materials Needed:

a variety of real seashells
a large pan of water

Directions:

Let the children handle the various shells. They can poke their fingers in where the creatures lived, notice how color changes in or out of the water, etc. Stress the variety of God's little creatures that live in shells.

Shell Art

Materials Needed:

a lot of small shells or shell pieces
glue
construction paper

Directions:

Give each child a sheet of construction paper. Use glue to write the child's name, the name of a sea creature, or another word of your choice on the child's paper. The children can glue the shells/shell pieces to the paper.

A Searching Game

Based on Genesis 1:20–23

The sea is his, for he made it . . .
(Psalm 95:5)

Read Genesis 1:20–23 to the children. Then let them play the game below.

Materials Needed:

one or more packages of
   marine animal crackers
plastic sandwich bags

Directions:

Divide the animal crackers, putting several in each sandwich bag, and hide the bags around the room before the children arrive. When ready, tell the children they are to "swim" around the room, keeping their hands together, until they find the lost sea creatures. When all have been found, have the children divide the crackers, name each type of creature, and then enjoy the crackers as a snack.

Sea Scenes

These are fun for the children to create and look great on a bulletin board.

Materials Needed:

one paper plate per child
fish and seashell shapes cut
   out of construction paper
glue
blue plastic wrap or cellophane

Directions:

1. Give each child a paper plate.

2. Let the children glue fish and seashell shapes to their paper plates.

3. Cover each plate with blue plastic wrap or cellophane.

4. Attach them to a bulletin board.

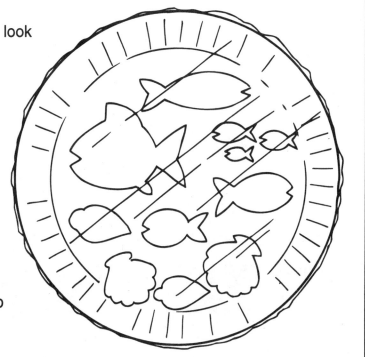

My Ocean Home
Based on Genesis 1:20–23

I will sing to the Lord all my life; I will sing praise to my God as long as I live. (Psalm 104:33)

Color the creature in each line that lives in the ocean.

Fantastic Fish

Based on Genesis 1:20–23

"For the earth will be filled with the knowledge of the glory of the Lord, as the waters cover the sea." (Habakkuk 2:14)

God gave us many beautiful fish to enjoy. He created fish on Day 5. Color the fish in the picture below.

Count the fish. Circle the number.

1   2   3   4   5   6   7   8

SS4883

Little Birdie Songs

Based on Genesis 1:20–23

Flowers appear on the earth; the season of singing has come, the cooing of doves is heard in our land. (Song of Songs 2:12)

Read Genesis 1:20–23 to the children, stressing the creation of birds. Talk with the children about birds they know. Then teach them the songs below.

Lots of Birds
(Tune: "Row, Row, Row Your Boat")

God made lots of birds

All for you and me!

Red and blue and big and small—

All pretty as can be!

Way Up High
(Tune: "Mary Had a Little Lamb")

I see birds fly way up high,

Way up high,

In the sky.

I see birds fly way up high.

I watch God's birds fly by.

God's Birds
(Tune: "My Bonnie Lies Over the Ocean")

God made birds fly over the dry land;   (Extend arms with hands waving.)

God made birds fly over the sea.

Some birds build their nests by the water,   (Hold two hands together like a nest. Then pretend to lean down towards water.)

And others build nests in a tree.   (Lift the nested hands high.)

Big birds, small birds,   (Measure with hands wide, then close.)

God's birds are all pretty to me, to me.   (Smile and hold hands to chest.)

Red birds, blue birds,   (Hold out one hand for each color.)

God's birds are all pretty to me.   (Nod and smile, as hands are held to chest.)

Birdhouse Greeting Card

Based on Genesis 1:20–23

Even the sparrow has found a home, and the swallow a nest for herself, where she may have her young—a place near your altar, O Lord Almighty, my King and my God. (Psalm 84:3)

These cards make the perfect gift for anyone who needs cheering up!

Materials Needed (per child):

half of a sheet of construction paper, ruler, pencil, paste, scissors, bird sticker

Directions:

1. Give each child half of a sheet of construction paper.

2. Have each child fold the paper in half to greeting card size.

3. On the front half, have them draw a rectangle.

4. Then they can cut three sides of the rectangle so that a flap is created. The flap will open like a door.

5. Help the children glue the front and back of the card together, except for the "door."

6. They can paste or stick the bird sticker so it will show when the flap is opened.

glue →

7. Help the children compose a greeting for the card, such as "Happy Birthday" or "Get Well Soon."

8. Print the greeting on the board so the children can copy it on the front of their cards. (If they are not able to do that yet, have them print their names on the back of the cards and write the greeting for them.)

Flying Bird Craft
Based on Genesis 1:20–23

Because you are my help, I sing in the shadow of your wings. (Psalm 63:7)

Discuss the birds the children see flying in your area. Then tell the children that they are going to make a bird that flies.

Materials Needed (per child):

construction paper
copy of the patterns below
brad fasteners
scissors
pencil
hole punch

Directions:

1. Help the children trace and cut out the patterns below on construction paper.

2. Show them how to use a brad to fasten a wing to each side of the bird's body so the wings can move. Have children "fly" their birds around the room and land on the chalk tray or a table.

3. Discuss with the children the things God gives birds to eat.

Alphabet Eagle

Based on Genesis 1:20–23

. . . those who hope in the Lord will renew their strength. They will soar on wings like eagles; they will run and not grow weary, they will walk and not be faint. (Isaiah 40:31)

Connect the dots from A–Z. What big bird did you make? Trace its name. Write it.

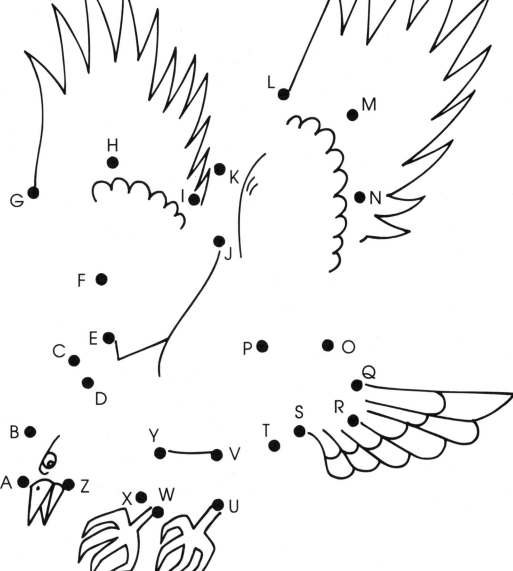

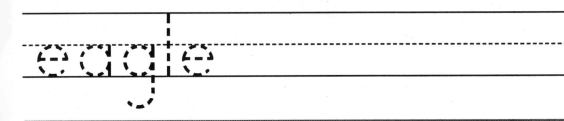

Different Birds

Based on Genesis 1:20–23

Sing to the Lord a new song; sing to the Lord, all the earth. (Psalm 96:1)

Each bird picture is a little different from the other. Find the differences. Color the part that is different.

Animal Fun

Based on Genesis 1:24–25

As the deer pants for streams of water, so my soul pants for you, O God. (Psalm 42:1)

Clay Animals

Read Genesis 1:24–25 to the children. Then tell them they can make little animals to look like the big wild ones God made.

Materials Needed:

modeling clay
pictures or toy samples of wild animals

Directions:

Give each child a piece of modeling clay or play dough. Show them pictures of wild animals or samples from a Noah's Ark set. Let each child choose, model, and identify the animal he or she makes. Children can then pretend to walk the animals on Noah's Ark, have an animal parade, or sing "Good Ole Noah Had an Ark" to the tune of "Old MacDonald Had a Farm," etc.

Animal Parade

This is a fun way for children to learn all about God's wonderful animals.

Materials Needed (per child):

paper bag large enough to go over each child's head, with large eye holes already cut out
crayons

Directions:

Tell the children that they can be any animal they want. Each one can draw his or her animal's face on the paper bag. Children can draw whiskers for lions and tigers, a trunk for an elephant, etc. When every child has his or her face ready, have the children put on their masks and parade around the room or perhaps into another classroom.

Name the Animals

Based on Genesis 1:24–25

How many are your works, O Lord! In wisdom you made them all; the earth is full of your creatures. (Psalm 104:24)

God made lots of wonderful animals. Some of them are below. Draw a line from each animal to its name.

sheep

pig

cow

horse

dog

donkey

cat

SS48835

Animal Homes

Based on Genesis 1:24–25

Blessed are those who dwell in your house; they are ever praising you. (Psalm 84:4)

God gave every animal a special home. Draw a line from each animal to its home.

37

God's Creepy Critters
Based on Genesis 1:24–25

Do you not know? Have you not heard? The Lord is the everlasting God, the Creator of the ends of the earth. (Isaiah 40:28)

Read Genesis 1:24–25 to the children. Explain to them that not all the living things God made are big. Some are very small. Then try the activities below with them.

Materials Needed:

ball of twine, box of colored cereal rings, scissors, twist ties of various lengths and colors, construction paper, glue, pipe cleaners, markers or crayons

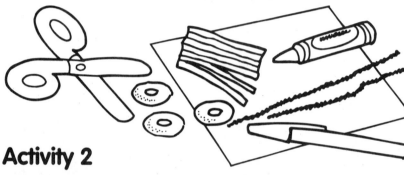

Activity 1

Show the children how to thread circles of cereal onto string to make "a creature that moves along the ground," like a caterpillar. See which children can make the most colorful creatures.

Activity 2

Tell the children that spiders have eight legs, four on each side, that they use to crawl around. Let each child pick four twist ties of the same length. Show them how to twist the centers together to make small bodies with extending legs. Talk about any spiders the children are familiar with.

Activity 3

Give the children construction paper they can use to cut out several of the same size circle—about 4"–5" in diameter. (You could perhaps show them how to fold a sheet of paper several times and cut through the layers to create the circles all at one time.) Have them draw a face on one of their circles and glue on two pipe cleaner pieces for antennae. Help the children glue their circles together to create a creepy critter caterpillar.

Hidden Animals

Based on Genesis 1:24–25

Let everything that has breath praise the Lord . . . (Psalm 150:6)

Find the animals hiding in the forest. Color each one a different color.

Dot-to-Dot Animal
Based on Genesis 1:24–25

Know that the Lord is God. It is he who made us, and we are his; we are his people, the sheep of his pasture. (Psalm 100:3)

Connect the dots from 1 to 20. When you finish, you will have an outline of an animal that God made. What animal is it?

Circle the name of the animal.

horse   sheep   cow   dog

© Shining Star Publications

SS48835

Day 6

Tame or Wild?

Based on Genesis 1:24–25

The wolf will live with the lamb, the leopard will lie down with the goat, the calf and the lion and the yearling together; and a little child will lead them. (Isaiah 11:6)

God made some animals tame—to be with people. He made some animals wild—to roam free through the land and trees. He made fish to swim in the waters, birds to fly in the air, and insects to crawl or fly.

Cross out the picture that does not belong in each line.

People Rhymes
Based on Genesis 1:26–31

The Lord gives strength to his people; the Lord blesses his people with peace. (Psalm 29:11)

Read Genesis 1:26–31 to the children. Explain that *image* means *a picture or statue or likeness in personality or spirit.* Then explain to the children what choral speaking is—talking together in a certain pattern. Then teach the children the action rhymes below.

I. **Girls:** In the *image of God*

          Doesn't mean just our face   *(Cover faces with hands.)*

  Boys: Or our two long arms   *(Stretch out arms.)*

          Or our feet.   *(Stretch out one foot.)*

  Unison: It means that He made us   *(Raise arms to chest and then toward heaven.)*

          With a spirit like His

  1 Girl: To be kind   *(Spread arms out to the sides.)*

  1 Boy: And help all whom we meet. *(Hug arms in close.)*

II. **Unison:** Boys and girls   *(Boys and girls point to each other.)*

           Are meant to be

  1 Girl: So much like God   *(Point to heaven.)*

  1 Boy: That people see   *(Cup hands around eyes.)*

  Boys: The plan and care

  Girls: That God provides   *(Point to heaven.)*

  Unison: For living things

           And all the world besides. *(Make a big circle with hands.)*

God's People

Based on Genesis 1:26–31

Who is he, this King of glory? The Lord Almighty—He is the King of glory. (Psalm 24:10)

Read Genesis 1:26–31 to the children. Explain to them that this song is about everything God made. Help them realize that God did not give people control over the lights in the sky or the water in the oceans—just the living things on land and in the sea. Then teach the children this song to the tune of "Itsy, Bitsy Spider."

God created people
To rule His land and seas,
His animals and birds
And fish and plants and trees.

God blessed the man and woman
And the world wherein they stood.
Then He saw His whole creation
Was very, very good.

People Dolls

These are fun for the children to create to remind them to be thankful for their families and friends.

Materials Needed:

one 9" x 5" strip of paper per child; scissors; glue; crayons or markers; decorative items (yarn, sequins, fabric scraps, ribbon, buttons, etc.); one copy of the pattern per child

Directions:

Help the children fold their strips three times. Show them how to lay their patterns on their folded strips and trace around them, making sure that the hands are on the folds. Help the children cut out their paper dolls. Make sure the children do not cut the hands apart. The children can then decorate their paper dolls to look like friends or family members.

Playing With God's People

Based on Genesis 1:26–31

I lift up my eyes to the hills—where does my help come from? My help comes from the Lord, the Maker of heaven and earth. (Psalm 121:1–2)

Read Genesis 1:26–31 to the children. Explain to them that there are many, many more people in the world now than when God first created man and woman. Today, there are many people of different sizes, colors, and occupations. Then let them try the activities below.

A People Collage
Materials Needed:
old magazines
scissors for each child
a large sheet of posterboard
paste

Directions:
Have children cut out pictures of people and make a collage by pasting all of them on one large sheet of posterboard. You can title the creation "God's Perfectly Wonderful People."

People Motion Play
Have the children stand in a circle. Then teach them the motion play below.

People here, people there,	(Put hand to forehead to shield eyes as you
People, people everywhere.	look to the right, and then to the left.)
God's people live in every nation,	(All join hands.)
For we are all God's great creation!	(Raise joined hands.)

God Did Make Us
(Tune: "London Bridge Is Falling Down")

Let the children sing the song together as a prayer.

God did make us one and all,

Big and small,

Short and tall.

God did make us

And we say

Thank You, Father.

Fingerpainting Creation
Based on Genesis 1:26–31

How many are your works, O Lord! In wisdom you made them all; the earth is full of your creatures. (Psalm 104:24)

Read Genesis 1:26–31 to the children. Talk with them about all the different things God created. Then let each child create a picture of something God created that he or she likes best.

Materials Needed:
finger paints
paper
scissors
paste/tape
long paper for display

Directions:
Give each child a sheet of paper and some paint and let the children work on their paintings. When the paintings have dried (probably after 24 hours or so), have each child cut out his or her picture and paste it onto a long sheet of mural paper along with the paintings of the other children. Tape this creation artwork to a wall or board. Now is a good time to sing the whole creation song (page 7).

For More Fun:
Let the children work in groups, with each group painting a creation scene on a large sheet of mural paper. You could give each group a list of things to include in its mural.

Painting Each Day
Divide the children into seven groups. Give each group a large sheet of mural paper. Assign each group a day of creation. Each group must fingerpaint what God created (or did) on its assigned day. Let the groups present their works of art, in chronological order, to parents or another class.

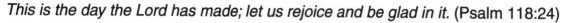

The Special Seventh Day

Based on Genesis 2:2–3

This is the day the Lord has made; let us rejoice and be glad in it. (Psalm 118:24)

Read Genesis 2:2–3 to the children. Then tell them that we should thank God especially for the seventh day, the day on which God rested after creating the world. Write the prayer below on the board. Ask the children to join hands and say it after you, line by line.

The Seventh Day

We thank You, God,
For the seventh day,
For time to rest,
And time to play,
For time to learn
And time to pray,
We thank You, God.

Children's Prayer

Ask each child what he or she would especially like to thank God for. List these things on the board and have the children all join hands and bow their heads as you pray in thanksgiving for all the things they have mentioned.

Let's Rest!

Create a bulletin board with the title, "Let's Rest . . . and Give Thanks to God!" Let the children cut out or draw pictures of things they do on Sundays to praise God. Discuss the pictures with the children before attaching them to the board.

Thankful Place Mats

Materials Needed:

one sheet of construction paper per child
glue
scissors
magazines

Directions:

Give each child a sheet of construction paper containing the title "Thank You, God, for . . ." The children can then cut out pictures of things God created for which they are thankful. Laminate the place mats if possible and let the children use them at snack time.

Thank You, God, for...

SS48835

A Super Seventh Day
Based on Genesis 2:2–3

Enter his gates with thanksgiving and his courts with praise; give thanks to him and praise his name. (Psalm 100:4)

Read Genesis 2:2–3 to the children and talk to them about the holiness of the seventh day, the ways we celebrate it, and how calendars remind us of this special day. Then let them try the activities below.

Seventh Day Bracelets
Materials Needed (per child):
old calendar page containing large numbers

one circle of construction paper, cut a little larger than the calendar squares

a piece of yarn

hole punch

paste

Directions:
Have each child cut out a square with a 7 on it. Then they paste the square on the circle. Help each child punch a hole in his or her circle, thread a piece of yarn through it, and tie it on his or her wrist.

Seven Days of Creation Strips
Materials Needed (per child):
old calendar page containing large numbers

scissors

glue

strips of construction paper

hole punch

yarn

Directions:
Explain to the children that you are going to help them make a decoration to hang in a window or on a lampshade at home. Have each child cut out squares containing the numbers 1–7 on them. Have the children paste the squares vertically on a strip of construction paper. Then help them punch a hole at the top and thread a piece of yarn through it to use to hang the decoration.

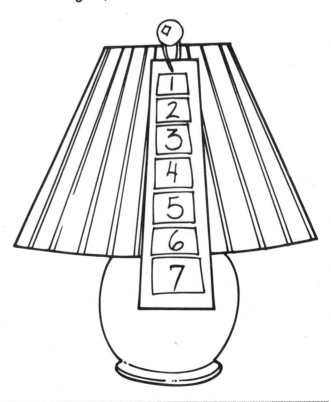

SS48835

A Creation Celebration

Based on Genesis 2:1–3

May the words of my mouth and the meditation of my heart be pleasing in your sight, O Lord, my Rock and my Redeemer. (Psalm 19:14)

Read Genesis 2:1–3 to the children. Remind them that celebrating often means having a party. Tell them that today, they are going to have a party to celebrate creation. Let the children make the cookies, drink the punch, and do the activities below to have a super Creation Celebration!

Creation Cookies

Materials Needed:

plain cookies
two or more cans of prepared
  frosting in different colors
plastic knives and toothpicks
a plate or serving tray
napkins

Directions:

Provide the children with the cookies and other materials. Discuss the many wonderful things God created with the children. Then let them spread frosting on each cookie and decorate it, making any design they want involving creation (examples—a star, an animal, a face, etc.).

Tasty Creation Drink

Make some blue Kool-Aid™ with the children. Find fish-shaped ice cubes and float them in the drink. Children can drink out of cups on which they paste pictures of God's sea creatures.

Fun and Games

Children may sing any of the songs, play any of the games, and perform any of the action rhymes relating to creation found throughout the book. For more fun, invite another class or parents to join the Creation Celebration.

SS48835